Accounting for Art Galleries

Steven M. Bragg

AccountingTools®

ISBN 978-1-64221-126-9

For more information about AccountingTools® products, visit our Web site at www.accountingtools.com.

Table of Contents

About the Author

Steven Bragg, CPA, has been the chief financial officer or controller of four companies, as well as a consulting manager at Ernst & Young. He received a master's degree in finance from Bentley College, an MBA from Babson College, and a Bachelor's degree in Economics from the University of Maine. He has been a two-time president of the Colorado Mountain Club, and is an avid alpine skier, mountain biker, and certified master diver. Mr. Bragg resides in Centennial, Colorado. He has written more than 300 books and courses, including *New Controller Guidebook*, *GAAP Guidebook*, and *Payroll Management*.

Steven maintains the accountingtools.com web site, which contains continuing professional education courses, the Accounting Best Practices podcast, and thousands of articles on accounting subjects.

Buy Additional AccountingTools Courses

AccountingTools offers more than 1,500 hours of CPE courses, with concentrations in accounting, auditing, finance, taxation, and ethics. Related courses that you might like include:

- Bookkeeping Guidebook
- Closing the Books

Go to accountingtools.com/cpe to view these additional courses.

AccountingTools®

Accounting for Art Galleries

Introduction

An *art gallery* is an outlet through which works of art are marketed. Art galleries are a key part of the social life of a city. They support many of the artists in the local area, and arrange exhibitions to make art available to collectors within the region. What they do might initially appear to be a high-class function that is buoyed by vast amounts of cash flow, but the reality is somewhat different. The typical gallery owner must deal with many of the same business issues experienced by a manufacturer or a distributor – and they are particularly prone to deep losses when the economy tanks. In this book, we will explore the essentials of art gallery operations, and then cover the accounting issues with which they must deal.

Art Gallery Revenue Structure

More than half of all art galleries earn less than $200,000 per year. Since roughly half of these revenues are then forwarded to artists in the form of commissions, this leaves quite a small amount of residual cash to pay for the other major expenses – rent, promotions, and wages. For these galleries, the financial situation is clearly dire, which leads to many gallery closures every year. An added concern is that many gallery owners are passionate about their craft, and so stay open longer than is prudent, running up substantial debts for several years before finally closing.

Conversely, about 15% of all galleries take in more than $1 million per year. These galleries are in the "sweet spot" of the industry, having attracted some of the best artists whose works sell for substantial premiums, as well as the collectors interested in buying their works.

The outcome of this revenue structure is substantial turnover among the smaller galleries, with a few of them – mostly due to their relationship development prowess – expanding their sales enough to enter into the much more stable top group of galleries.

Art Gallery Competitors

Art galleries are faced with a great deal of competition. This comes from the artists, who can avoid the 50% gallery commission by selling direct to collectors (hence the proliferation of artist websites and their very active Instagram presence). There are also other galleries, which are always interested in poaching both the best artists and collectors. Auction houses are increasingly interested in taking over the sale of collections from the estates of deceased collectors, which used to be a profitable gallery niche. And finally, some artists have chosen to sell through online art platforms, which demand vastly smaller commissions for their services.

Art Gallery Marketing Principles

A successful art gallery adheres to a number of marketing principles in order to be consistently profitable. These principles are:

- *Coherent collection.* The gallery should adhere to a specific vision for what is to be presented, so that only certain types of works are made available. This approach results in a specific group of clients returning to the gallery, because they know roughly what they will find there.
- *Relationship development.* The mainstay of art gallery marketing is developing and maintaining relationships, both with artists and clients. Doing so ensures a continuing supply of artwork to the gallery, and a continuing stream of purchases from it.
- *Presentation excellence.* Perfect presentation of artwork translates into an impression of value, which leads to higher prices. Consequently, a successful gallery will not stack an excessive number of paintings in its display space, will provide sufficient lighting, and will ensure that the premises are immaculately clean.

The more successful galleries focus more on the art than the business. These gallery owners realize that the most passionate collectors (who happen to be the ones willing to spend the most) are attracted to great art, well presented – so that is what they provide.

One of the previous bullet points was relationship development. While it is certainly true that a majority of this development time needs to be spent with clients (the sales side of the business), a large amount also has to be devoted to artists (the supplier side of the business). Some artists have developed their own brands and are actively engaged in self-promotion. These artists require little hand holding, but others have no interest in this most crucial part of the business, and so will require substantially more assistance from the gallery to make them known to and appreciated by collectors.

An unusual point in regard to sales is that many of the works at an exhibition have been pre-sold – usually to long-standing customers who were contacted by the gallery well in advance of the exhibition's opening date. It is quite rare for an unknown buyer to appear at an opening and make a purchase. One might reasonably wonder why a gallery would hold an exhibition when the works are not even available for sale. The reason is publicity – the featured artist's work may appear in a news article, and his or her work will be available for viewing by potential new collectors.

Art Collectors

Art collectors are the largest source of revenue for a gallery, so it can be useful to break them down into categories. Each of these groups has a different lifetime value, as we will see in the following bullet points:

- *Art lovers.* These are the most passionate collectors, and are continually searching for valued additions to their collections. They have a high lifetime value to the gallery, and are considered the cornerstone of its success.
- *One-time buyers.* As the name implies, these parties are looking for a particular piece, usually to fulfill a decoration need within their homes. Their lifetime values are much lower than for art lovers.
- *Dealers.* These parties are looking for pieces that they can resell. They tend to be quite picky, looking for works that will appeal to their clients and to which they can apply their own markup. They may have a high lifetime value, but they also negotiate for lower prices, and so represent a lower profit margin.
- *Investors.* These individuals buy art as an investment and then hold it with the intention of a later sale, once the price has appreciated. They are highly selective buyers, looking for artists whose works are just catching on, and so are relatively undervalued.
- *Museums.* These entities buy art for their permanent collections. They are likely pursuing the works of specific artists, and so may only appear for the occasional purchase. Their lifetime value tends to be low.
- *Corporate collectors.* These parties are looking for artwork to display in their headquarters and other facilities. They may buy in bulk, but will also demand a discount in exchange for their volume purchases. Their lifetime value tends to be low.

Art Gallery Operations

Art galleries are mostly smaller establishments, usually operated by the gallery owner and perhaps a few part-time staff who are not especially well paid. This is typically the state of affairs for the first few years, while the owner acquires reputable artists and develops a roster of valued clients. Over time, the owner expands into progressively larger locations, typically in the higher-rent districts that collectors are more likely to frequent. As part of the expansion process, the owner assigns various roles to his or her staff. The archivist maintains the records of the artists working with the gallery; these records include the artist's works, sales, exhibitions, press, awards, and so forth. The registrar receives, documents, and manages the storage, conservation, and preservation of all artwork moving through the gallery's inventory. This person also prepares condition reports when receiving artwork so that this information can be sent to any client who buys the artwork. The gallery also employs sales staff, who are available to answer any questions from visitors, acquire contact information, and gently nudge them into buying artwork. The sales staff may work on a base-plus-commission basis, with the best ones earning substantial incomes.

A significant part of art gallery operations now involves art fairs, which are held around the world at essentially any location where the wealthier clients are likely to congregate. If a gallery is accepted into a fair (not an easy task), it must then pay a substantial up-front fee for booth space, pay to have a selection of its artworks transported there (and back), and incur the travel and entertainment costs required to send staff to the fair. There is also an increased staffing cost, since someone has to oversee the gallery while most of the staff is attending fairs. While very expensive, the best fairs can be quite profitable for a gallery, and represent a great opportunity to expand its client list.

Artist Relations

A gallery typically agrees to represent a modest number of artists. These arrangements are quite valuable for both parties. The artist gains a sales outlet and so can concentrate on developing new works of art. In addition, the gallery agrees to conduct an exhibition for the artist, usually once every two years, which it promotes to its client list. These exhibitions are highly valued by artists, since they can gain broader exposure to buyers, which drives up the prices of their artwork. If an artist is struggling financially, a generous gallery may even pay the person a small stipend, and buy a few works outright.

In exchange for these services, the gallery enters into a consignment arrangement with the artist, where the parties take a 50/50 split of all sales generated by the gallery. This means that the artist continues to own the works displayed in the gallery, so that the gallery does not take on the up-front risk of buying any artwork. If an artist becomes quite successful, this split may change somewhat, though the artist rarely takes more than 60% of the sale price. This arrangement has a few other features, including the following (all of which are negotiable):

- The artist is responsible for packaging artwork to be delivered to the gallery, while the gallery pays for the shipping.
- If the gallery cannot sell artwork, it asks the artist to take it back, thereby clearing out display and storage space that can be used for other artwork.
- The gallery pays for framing costs once a painting arrives at the gallery from the artist. The gallery can then deduct the cost of the framing from the proceeds of a painting sale, prior to calculating the commission split. If the artist insists on doing the framing, then the gallery reimburses the artist for the cost of the frame before calculating the commission split.

The Secondary Market

An alternative form of art acquisition for a gallery owner is to buy art on the secondary market. This means making purchases at estate sales and auctions, as well as by acquiring artwork from private collections or from other galleries. This is done whenever the gallery owner believes that artwork is being offered at below-market prices, and especially when the owner believes that he or she can flip it to a client within a relatively short period of time. If used prudently, this approach can yield significant profits, especially when an owner limits these acquisitions to the works of artists for whom there is already an established market.

A variation on the concept is to represent the estates of deceased artists, sometimes by winning over executors. The gallery owner can then develop exhibitions that emphasize the historical context in which the artworks of deceased artists can be placed, which will attract certain types of collectors. At an expanded level, a gallery can even represent the estates of multiple deceased artists whose works are connected in some way. Eventually, the gallery can become known for being the go-to source for the works of specific deceased artists.

The downside of dabbling in the secondary market is the amount of capital needed, since artwork is almost always acquired for cash. This means that the gallery will require vastly more working capital than would otherwise be the case. In addition, this presents an inventory risk, since some of these works may be held for months or even years, and may prove to be unsellable – or at least at the price points set by the gallery owner.

The Economic Entity Principle

Before we delve into the details of the accounting for art galleries, an essential topic to address is the economic entity principle. This principle states that the recorded activities of a business entity (such as an art gallery) should be kept separate from the recorded activities of its owners. This means that the accountant must maintain separate accounting records and bank accounts for the gallery, and not intermix them with the assets and liabilities of the owner. This is a particular concern with art galleries, which tend to be small and operated by a sole proprietor. The gallery owner may forget to separate personal expenditures from those of the gallery, resulting in payments being made from the gallery checking account to pay for personal expenditures.

One of the most common violations of this principle is in regard to the personal ownership of artwork. A gallery owner, being a connoisseur, may feel entirely justified in buying pieces for his or her own personal enjoyment, and may even store or display them at the gallery. These expenditures are separate from the purview of the gallery, and so should not be included in the accounting records of the gallery in any way. The money of the gallery should not be used to acquire them, and they should not appear in its inventory records.

Journal Entry Overview

Through the remainder of this book, we will insert examples of journal entries that show how to account for certain types of transactions. So, before going any further, we need to describe what a journal entry is and how it works. A journal entry is a formalized method for recording a business transaction. It is recorded in the accounting records of a business, known as the general ledger. A *general ledger* is the master set of accounts that summarize all transactions occurring within a business.

Journal entries are used in a double entry accounting system, where the intent is to record every business transaction in at least two places. For example, when a gallery sells a painting for cash, this increases both the revenue account and the cash account. Or, if framing stock is purchased on account, this increases both the accounts payable account and the inventory account.

The structure of a journal entry is:

- A header line may include a journal entry number and entry date.
- The first column includes the account number and account name into which the entry is recorded. This field is indented if it is for the account being credited.
- The second column contains the debit amount to be entered.
- The third column contains the credit amount to be entered.
- A footer line may also include a brief description of the reason for the entry.

Thus, the basic journal entry format is:

	Debit	Credit
Account name / number	$xx,xxx	
Account name / number		$xx,xxx

The structural rules of a journal entry are that there must be a minimum of two line items in the entry, and that the total amount entered in the debit column equals the total amount entered in the credit column.

A journal entry is usually printed and stored in a binder of accounting transactions, with backup materials attached that justify the entry. This information may be accessed by the gallery's auditors as part of their annual audit activities.

There are several types of journal entries, including:

- *Adjusting entry*. An adjusting entry is used at month-end to alter the financial statements to bring them into compliance with the relevant accounting standards. For example, a gallery could accrue unpaid wages at month-end in order to recognize the wages expense in the current period.
- *Compound entry*. This is a journal entry that includes more than two lines of entries. It is frequently used to record complex transactions, or several transactions at once. For example, the journal entry to record a payroll usually contains many lines, since it involves the recordation of numerous tax liabilities and payroll deductions.
- *Reversing entry*. This is an adjusting entry that is reversed as of the beginning of the following period, usually because an expense was accrued in the preceding period, and is no longer needed. Thus, a wage accrual in the preceding period is reversed in the next period, to be replaced by an actual payroll expenditure.

In general, journal entries are not used to record high-volume transactions, such as client billings or supplier invoices. These transactions are handled through specialized software modules within the accounting software that present a standard on-line form to be filled out. Once the form is complete, the software automatically creates the accounting record.

Sources of Revenue

The vast majority of all art gallery revenue comes – predictably – from the sale of artwork. However, galleries supplement this revenue by charging for the following additional services:

- *Artist catalogs.* The gallery may choose to prepare artist catalogs and hand them out at exhibitions, or charge for them. In the latter case, this tends to be quite a minor source of revenue.
- *Brokering of repair services.* A client reports damage to artwork, so the gallery arranges to have it shipped back for repair work, either by the artist or a conservator.
- *Commissions on the sale of artwork.* A client may ask a gallery to sell some of the client's artwork for a commission, which is usually around 20%.
- *Framing services.* The gallery charges for framing work requested by clients.
- *Home delivery and hanging services.* The gallery arranges not only for shipment to clients (which is sometimes free) but also for hanging services within the homes of clients (which is not free).
- *Rental of exhibition space.* Though most galleries are not large, they can be considered quite stylish places for private receptions, talks, dinners, and so forth.

A key element of revenue is the price point charged to customers. The gallery owner tries to avoid any hint of a discount, since this reduces the perceived value of an artwork. Nonetheless, discounts are discreetly offered to long-term collectors, while volume discounts may be offered if several works are acquired at the same time. Also, if art has not moved for an extended period of time, a gallery may offer unadvertised price reductions in order to clear them from stock. In addition, museums may insist on a hefty discount – which may be worth it if the result is having an artist's work be prominently displayed in the museum.

If a gallery has signed an exclusive representation agreement with an artist, the contract may state that the gallery receives a fee if the artist's works are sold elsewhere within the territory established for the exclusive use of the gallery. For example, if an artist wants to show in another gallery in the designated sales region for the primary gallery, the primary gallery is owed 20% of the sale price. Or, if the artist wants to terminate a formal agreement with a gallery and be represented elsewhere, the agreement may mandate that the original gallery is to receive a commission on sales of the artist's works at the successor gallery for a period of time, such as one year.

EXAMPLE

Cold Smoke Gallery needs to account for several revenue-related transactions that have occurred during the past month. First, it sells a sculpture for $8,000, paid for with a credit card, for which there is a 50/50 revenue split arrangement with the sculptor. The revenue portion of the entry, ignoring all sales tax issues, is:

	Debit	Credit
Cash (asset)	7,760	
Credit card fees (expense)	240	
Revenue – sculptures (revenue)		8,000

Next, the accountant pays the sculptor his 50% commission on the sale, using the following entry:

	Debit	Credit
Commissions (expense)	4,000	
Cash (asset)		4,000

[There is also an inventory component to this sale, for which examples are provided later in the Artwork Inventory section]

Next, a painting owned by a client suffers moderate water damage as the result of a fire at the client's home, and the client asks the gallery to send it back to the artist for repair work. For this brokering service, the gallery earns a $2,500 fee, for which it bills the client. The entry is:

	Debit	Credit
Accounts receivable (asset)	2,500	
Revenue – repair brokering (revenue)		2,500

Finally, a local business group rents out the exhibition space in the gallery for a formal dinner party. The gallery bills the business group a $3,000 rental fee. The entry is:

	Debit	Credit
Accounts receivable (asset)	3,000	
Revenue – space rental (revenue)		3,000

The Art Gallery Invoice

An *invoice* is a document submitted to a client, identifying a sale transaction for which the client owes payment to the gallery. A gallery invoice is somewhat more involved than an invoice created in other industries, since it includes additional information pertaining to the artwork being sold. The contents of a gallery's invoice include the following:

- Invoice number
- The date on which the sale occurred
- Client information, including the name, billing address, and shipping address (if different)
- Full details of the purchased artwork, including the following:
  - Artwork identification number
  - Title of the artwork
  - Artist name
  - Date of artwork completion
  - Dimensions
  - Number in edition
  - Thumbnail image of the artwork
- Price, including any discount granted
- Shipping charges
- Sales taxes
- Total price
- Terms of sale, such as payable on receipt or within 30 days
- Wire transfer information
- Additional statements, such as:
  - Title does not pass until full payment is received
  - Responsibility for insurance while the artwork is in transit
  - Copyright of the artwork remains the property of the artist

Many clients want this invoice to be sent to them in electronic format, along with a high-quality JPG of the artwork, which they can then insert into their own artwork tracking databases.

Sales Taxes

The charging of sales taxes is a significant issue for art galleries, since the amounts associated with a single sale of artwork can be substantial. Also, because of the concept of economic nexus, larger sales to clients located in other states may trigger an obligation to remit sales taxes to the applicable state government. We deal with these issues in the following sub-sections.

Sales Tax Accounting

When a client is billed for sales taxes, the journal entry is a debit to the accounts receivable asset for the entire amount of the invoice, a credit to the sales account for that portion of the invoice attributable to goods or services billed, and a credit to the sales tax liability account for the amount of sales taxes billed.

At the end of the month (or longer, depending on the remittance arrangement with the applicable state government), the accountant fills out a sales tax remittance form that states gross sales and sales taxes and sends the government the amount of the sales tax recorded in the sales tax liability account. This remittance may take place before the client has paid the gallery for the sales tax. When the client pays the invoice, the accountant debits the cash account for the amount of the payment and credits the accounts receivable account.

EXAMPLE

Cold Smoke Gallery issues an invoice to a client for a $5,000 sculpture, on which there is a seven percent sales tax. The entry is:

	Debit	Credit
Accounts receivable (asset)	5,350	
Revenue – sculptures (revenue)		5,000
Sales tax liability (liability)		350

Following the end of the month, Cold Smoke remits the sales taxes withheld to the state government. The entry is:

	Debit	Credit
Sales tax liability (liability)	350	
Cash (asset)		350

Later in the following month, the client pays the full amount of the invoice. The entry is:

	Debit	Credit
Cash (asset)	5,350	
Accounts receivable (asset)		5,350

A few states allow a business to retain a small portion of its sales tax collections as a discount. This discount is only made available if the firm remits payments on a timely basis.

Sales Tax Nexus

Nexus is the physical presence of a business in a state. Whenever nexus can be established, the gallery must charge clients for taxes related to that taxing authority and remit the collected taxes to the taxing entity. Given the multitude of taxing entities in the United States, it makes sense to minimize nexus, thereby reducing the number of tax remittance and reporting obligations of the gallery. As a general rule, an out-of-state gallery will have nexus in a state if it has regular and systematic contacts within the state, primarily through its employees, agents, or property. More specifically, nexus is considered to have been established if any one of the following conditions can be proven:

- A gallery maintains a facility of any type within the borders of the state, such as a warehouse or office.
- A gallery pays the wages of an employee located within the borders of the state.
- Gallery employees travel to the state to solicit business there, such as flying in to meet with a client.

Some taxing authorities have expanded the definition of nexus in order to generate more tax revenue. Their view includes the preceding items, plus the use of a gallery's own vehicles to transport artwork inside the borders of the taxing authority. Another possibility is economic nexus, which is covered in a later section.

Given these differences in what constitutes nexus, it is best to contact the local state government for the applicable rules regarding it.

Tax Remittances Required Under Nexus

If nexus exists, a gallery must take the following steps:

- File with the local state government to do business within the state, which requires a small annual filing fee
- Apply for a state sales tax license
- Withhold sales taxes on all sales made within the region
- Remit the sales taxes to the applicable government entity
- Pay personal property taxes on any assets located within the region

Nexus Avoidance

The main effect of nexus is that it requires a significant amount of time by the accountant to keep track of tax rates, adjust client billings, and remit taxes. These activities can add to the administrative headcount, so there is general resistance to having nexus applied to a gallery by yet another taxing authority. Nexus avoidance can even be an active planning process that may include the avoidance of gallery-owned delivery vehicles and avoiding the use of facilities in certain states that are known for being particularly aggressive about collecting sales taxes.

Economic Nexus

The Supreme Court handed down a major decision involving sales taxes in 2018, where it stated in the *South Dakota vs. Wayfair* case that South Dakota could apply its sales tax to Internet retailers, even when they have no property or employees in the state. The Court was ruling specifically on the South Dakota sales tax law, pointing out that this law was no burden to interstate commerce, given that it did not impose an obligation to remit sales taxes retroactively and imposed a simplified tax rate structure.

The Wayfair case means that the concept of *economic nexus* is now a major issue for anyone selling to customers located in another state. Economic nexus is created when a gallery generates a certain amount of sales in a particular state. Some state governments measure this figure based on the overall dollar amount of transactions generated, while others combine the concept with the total number of individual sales transactions completed. It is an open question as to how low a state can go in setting economic nexus thresholds, since very low thresholds make it more difficult for small galleries to administer.

The ramifications of economic nexus are clearly more administrative work for any gallery that sells across state lines (such as any gallery with clients located in other states). This is not especially difficult when a state provides galleries with a consolidated application and administration system, but this is not always the case – some states have quite a disorganized approach to economic nexus, requiring sellers to make separate filings with individual cities and counties. Calculating sales tax is a particular concern in the latter case, where a gallery may have to deal with hundreds or even thousands of different sales tax rates. Individual states are still deciding how to handle the economic nexus concept. The following table shows the current status of the situation in each state.

Economic Nexus Rules by State[1]

State	Current Status	Threshold Level(s)	Includable Sales
Alabama	In effect	$250,000	Retail sales
Alaska	Only City of Nome	$100,000 **and** 100 transactions	Gross sales
Arizona	In effect	$150,000 in 2020 and $100,000 in 2021	Gross sales
Arkansas	In effect	$100,000 **or** 200 transactions	Taxable sales
California	In effect	$500,000	Gross sales
Colorado	In effect	$100,000	Retail sales
Connecticut	In effect	$100,000 **and** 200 transactions	Gross sales
District of Columbia	In effect	$100,000 **or** 200 transactions	Retail sales
Florida	In effect	$100,000	Taxable sales
Georgia	In effect	$100,000 **or** 200 transactions	Retail sales
Hawaii	In effect	$100,000 **or** 200 transactions	Gross sales
Idaho	In effect	$100,000	Gross sales
Illinois	In effect	$100,000 **or** 200 transactions	Retail sales
Indiana	In effect	$100,000 **or** 200 transactions	Gross sales
Iowa	In effect	$100,000 **or** 200 transactions	Gross sales
Kansas	In effect	$100,000	Gross sales
Kentucky	In effect	$100,000 **or** 200 transactions	Retail sales
Louisiana	In effect	$100,000 **or** 200 transactions	Gross sales
Maine	In effect	$100,000 **or** 200 transactions	Gross sales
Maryland	In effect	$100,000 **or** 200 transactions	Gross sales
Massachusetts	In effect	$100,000	Gross sales
Michigan	In effect	$100,000 **or** 200 transactions	Gross sales
Minnesota	In effect	$100,000 **or** 200 transactions	Retail sales
Mississippi	In effect	$250,000+	Gross sales
Missouri	In effect	$100,000	Taxable sales
Nebraska	In effect	$100,000 **or** 200 transactions	Gross sales
Nevada	In effect	$100,000 **or** 200 transactions	Retail sales
New Jersey	In effect	$100,000 **or** 200 transactions	Retail sales
New Mexico	In effect	$100,000	Taxable sales
New York	In effect	$500,000 **and** 100 transactions	Gross sales
North Carolina	In effect	$100,000 **or** 200 transactions	Gross sales
North Dakota	In effect	$100,000	Taxable sales

---

[1] Information summarized from https://www.salestaxinstitute.com/resources/economic-nexus-state-guide

State	Current Status	Threshold Level(s)	Includable Sales
Ohio	In effect	$100,000 **or** 200 transactions	Gross sales
Oklahoma	In effect	$100,000	Taxable sales
Pennsylvania	In effect	$100,000	Gross sales
Rhode Island	In effect	$100,000 **or** 200 transactions	Taxable sales
South Carolina	In effect	$100,000	Gross sales
South Dakota	In effect	$100,000 **or** 200 transactions	Gross sales
Tennessee	In effect	$500,000	Retail sales
Texas	In effect	$500,000	Gross sales
Utah	In effect	$100,000 **or** 200 transactions	Taxable sales
Vermont	In effect	$100,000 **or** 200 transactions	Gross sales
Virginia	In effect	$100,000 **or** 200 transactions	Retail sales
Washington	In effect	$100,000	Retail sales
West Virginia	In effect	$100,000 **or** 200 transactions	Gross sales
Wisconsin	In effect	$100,000 **or** 200 transactions	Gross sales
Wyoming	In effect	$100,000 **or** 200 transactions	Gross sales

The preceding table does not include states that do not charge a sales tax. The driving factor for most galleries will be the dollar limit (usually $100,000), rather than the number of transactions (usually 200).

This means that a gallery will need to start compiling all sales transactions by state, and reviewing it on a monthly basis. The exact rules will vary by state, but assume that sales tax withholdings will need to begin as soon as $100,000 of sales have been completed within a calendar year.

EXAMPLE

Cold Smoke Gallery has sold two paintings to customers located in Ohio, for which the total sales amount is $99,999. It is August 13. Cold Smoke needs to start withholding sales tax on any additional sales to customers in Ohio, and remitting the proceeds to the state. Now that the $100,000 transaction threshold has been reached, Cold Smoke will need to withhold sales taxes on *all* sales into Ohio on a go-forward basis.

A further concern regarding economic nexus is that some states require sales taxes to be paid based on local sales tax rates where individual customers are located, rather than allowing out-of-state sellers to pay a single state-wide rate. This greatly amplifies the sales tax reporting burden, especially for galleries that have barely exceeded the sales thresholds needed to trigger sales tax withholding in most states.

The Accounts Receivable Aging Report

A great many gallery sales are made on-the-spot with a credit card, resulting in no accounts receivable. Nonetheless, there are still many situations in which an invoice may be needed. For example, a long-term client requests delayed payment terms for a particularly expensive piece of artwork. Or, the gallery bills a client for repair work on a damaged painting. Another option is a billing to a local business that wants to rent the gallery space for a private function. Because of these billings, it is essential for the gallery owner to keep track of unpaid accounts receivable. This is done with the accounts receivable aging report, which lists unpaid client invoices by date range. Given its use as a collection tool, the report may be configured to also contain contact information for each customer.

A typical aging report lists invoices in 30-day "buckets," where the columns contain the following information:

- The left-most column contains all invoices that are 30 days old or less
- The next column contains invoices that are 31-60 days old
- The next column contains invoices that are 61-90 days old
- The final column contains all older invoices

The report is sorted by client name, with all invoices for each client itemized directly below the client name, usually sorted by either invoice number or invoice date. A sample report follows, though without the individual invoice detail that is usually found in such a report.

Sample Accounts Receivable Aging Report

Client Name	Total Receivable	0-30 Days	31-60 Days	61-90 Days	90+ Days
Anderson, Michelle	$15,000	$10,000	$5,000		
Bufford, Abigail	29,000		20,000	$9,000	
Chesterton, Davis	83,000	47,000	21,000	12,000	$3,000
Denver Art Museum	8,000				8,000
Totals	$135,000	$57,000	$46,000	$21,000	$11,000

If the report is generated by an accounting software package, it may be possible to reconfigure the report for different date ranges. For example, if the gallery's payment terms are net 15 days, then the date range in the left-most column should only be for the first 15 days. This drops 16-day old invoices into the second column, which highlights that they are now overdue for payment.

Artwork Inventory

An essential point regarding art galleries is that the inventory it holds may be either on consignment or owned. It is usually on consignment when the gallery is directly representing an artist, though in some cases the gallery may buy artwork directly from artists, either as a way to provide them with immediate financial support, or because the gallery owner wants to buy the artwork of an up-and-coming artist whose works have a strong chance of appreciating in value over time. In the latter case, the gallery owner warehouses the acquired works, while working to build client recognition of the artist. Once the artist is reasonably well-known, the gallery owner gradually sells off his or her earlier acquisitions at greatly marked-up prices. Sales are generally trickled out over a period of time in order to control supply, thereby keeping prices high. Artwork is also owned by a gallery when it buys and sells artwork on the secondary market, as noted earlier in this book.

In short, keep in mind during the following discussion of inventory that some artwork will be recorded within an inventory at zero cost, because it is on consignment, and the system is merely being used to keep track of the artwork – not to keep track of its cost. Other artwork is directly owned by the gallery, so its full acquisition cost will be stated in the inventory records.

Given the unique nature of artwork, it is nearly always accounted for using the *specific identification method*. The principle requirements of this method are:

- Be able to track each inventory item individually. The easiest method is a paper label that contains a unique identification number.
- Be able to track the cost of each item individually. The accounting system should clearly identify the cost of each purchased item and associate it with a unique identification number.
- Be able to relieve inventory for the specific cost associated with an inventory item when it is sold.

The specific identification method introduces a high degree of accuracy to the cost of inventory, since the exact cost at which an artwork was purchased can be recorded in the inventory records and charged to the cost of goods sold when the related item is sold. This should include the cost of any framing and restoration work.

EXAMPLE

Cold Smoke Gallery acquires a landscape by Albert B. Chisholm at auction for $50,000, resulting in the following entry:

	Debit	Credit
Inventory – abc2020-001 (asset)	50,000	
Cash (asset)		50,000

In the entry, note that the inventory entry is targeted at the specific Chisholm painting. In this case, the "abc2020-001" denotes the initials of the artist, followed by the year in which the painting was acquired and then a sequential number for works acquired by the gallery for the artist in that year.

The gallery owner notices that there is some wear in one corner of the painting, as well as a small amount of water damage. She sends it to a nearby restoration specialist for repairs, resulting in the following entry for the restorer's $3,000 fee:

	Debit	Credit
Inventory – abc2020-001 (asset)	3,000	
Cash (asset)		3,000

Finally, she pays $1,000 to a local framing shop to create a frame for the painting, resulting in the following entry:

	Debit	Credit
Inventory – abc2020-001 (asset)	1,000	
Cash (asset)		1,000

Through this series of entries, $54,000 of expenditures have been specifically linked to the Chisholm painting. The gallery then sells the landscape to a client for $80,000 in cash, which results in the following two entries; the first entry removes the painting from inventory and charges it to the cost of goods sold expense, while the second entry records the associated revenue:

	Debit	Credit
Cost of goods sold (expense)	54,000	
Inventory – abc2020-001 (asset)		54,000

	Debit	Credit
Cash (asset)	80,000	
Revenue – Paintings (revenue)		80,000

There are a number of software packages that handle all of the requirements of an art gallery – one element of which is inventory tracking. These packages contain a number of additional fields not found in a more generic inventory tracking system. The fields typically included in an inventory record in these systems are as follows:

- *Identification number.* This uniquely identifies each artwork, usually by including the artist's initials, the year of the work, and a sequential number for works produced within that year. Thus, the second work of the year sent to the gallery by artist John Doe Smith in the year 2020 would have the identification number jds2020-002.
- *Title.* This the official name of the artwork.
- *Description.* This open-format field is especially useful when the work does not have a formal name, and needs to instead be described more generally.
- *Dimensions.* This is the full dimensions of the artwork.

- *Artist name.* This is the full name of the artist who created the artwork.
- *Year created.* This is the year in which the artist created the artwork.
- *Condition.* This is a statement of the condition of the artwork.
- *Consignment flag.* This is a flag that states whether an item is on consignment or is owned by the gallery. This is a key field, since it either allows one to enter the acquisition cost of an artwork (if purchased) or not (if on consignment).
- *Consignment duration.* This is the period of time that a consigned artwork has been held by the gallery. The gallery owner wants to track this time period, in order to decide whether to return unsold art to the artist, leaving room for newer pieces.
- *Location.* This is the current location of the work, such as a specific bin within a storage location, or the location to which it was loaned, or the collector to which it was sold.
- *Special instructions.* This is information about the suggested installation and care of the artwork.
- *Provenance.* This is the identification of from whom the artwork was acquired.
- *Retail price.* This is the price established for the artwork by the gallery.
- *Appraised value.* This is the appraised value of the artwork, preferably including the name of the appraiser and the date of the appraisal.
- *Insurance value.* This the amount at which the artwork was insured.
- *Photo.* This field contains a JPG photo of the artwork.
- *Associated expenses.* This may include framing charges, repair costs, shipping, and photographer fees.

EXAMPLE

The Cold Smoke Gallery receives a new work from the well-known artist Jessie Klara Longhorn; this is the fourth painting that the gallery has received from her this year. This work is on consignment, so Longhorn remains the owner. Cold Smoke's staff enters the artwork in its inventory system, turning on the consignment flag to indicate that the gallery does not own it. The gallery then provides a frame for the painting at a cost of $400, which it records in the inventory record with the following entry:

	Debit	Credit
Inventory – jkl2020-004 (asset)	400	
Cash (asset)		400

Later, the gallery sells the painting to a client, at which point the inventory-related portion of the transaction is as follows, where the inventory asset is charged to the cost of goods sold:

	Debit	Credit
Cost of goods sold (expense)	400	
Inventory – jkl2020-004 (asset)		400

There is an accounting requirement that artwork be recorded at the lower of its cost or market value. This can be a nearly impossible chore for an art gallery, since most of its works are unique, making it exceedingly difficult to determine their fair market value. The best situation in which fair market value can be determined is when there are multiple copies of an artwork on the market (such as a limited edition print run), and the gallery owner has access to the prices at which the other copies are selling. However, even in this case, the condition of the copies that have been sold may vary from those held by the gallery, making it more difficult to determine their fair market value.

EXAMPLE

Cold Smoke Gallery owns one copy of a limited edition print by famed Hawaiian artist Naia O. Paiva. Of the other 99 copies in existence, three have recently come up for sale on an on-line auction market, selling for an average of $3,750 each. Cold Smoke acquired its copy for $5,000. Cold Smoke's owner considers her copy to be equivalent in condition to the ones that were sold, so the indicated fair value seems reasonable. Accordingly, she creates the following entry to write down the cost of the print to its market value:

	Debit	Credit
Loss on LCM adjustment (expense)	1,250	
Inventory – nop2020-007 (asset)		1,250

Art Gallery Expenses

An art gallery incurs not only the usual expenses experienced by most small businesses, but also some quite unique ones. We list them all in alphabetical order in the following bullet points:

- *Advertising.* This is primarily used to make the public aware of upcoming exhibitions, and will vary, depending on the types of artwork that will be included in each one. Upper-end galleries can spend massive amounts in this area.
- *Art advisor fees.* An art advisor works with collectors to locate artworks that are most appropriate for their collections. If an art advisor acquires an artwork

on behalf of a client, the gallery typically pays the advisor a commission of 10-20%.

- *Art fairs.* A gallery may participate in art fairs, in which case it must rent space at the fair, and pay for the transport of artwork to and from the fair. Rental space at art fairs can be shockingly expensive.
- *Artist per diems.* A gallery may offer its artists a per diem payment when they are attending an art fair where the gallery is exhibiting their works.
- *Artist stipends.* In rare cases, a gallery may choose to pay an artist a stipend in order to focus his or her attention on the full-time creation of art.
- *Banking fees.* This is the fees charged by the bank to maintain a savings and checking account, as well as check deposit fees and so forth.
- *Benefits.* Wages are so low in this industry that some gallery owners try to make up for it with somewhat elevated benefits offerings.
- *Catalogs.* The gallery owner may elect to produce a catalog of an artist's works, usually just prior to an exhibit featuring that artist. These catalogs may be sold, in which case there is offsetting revenue.
- *Charitable contributions.* Given the connections that a gallery owner needs to develop, it is quite likely that contributions to local charities will be relatively high. The gallery may even donate owned artwork to a charity.
- *Commissions.* The typical gallery owner is holding the art works of its artists on consignment, and then pays a 50% commission to the artist if a work is sold. Usually, the agreement is for a commission to be payable within 30 days of the gallery's receipt of cash from a customer.
- *Crating.* The gallery will need to pay for crating, which is typically performed by an art handling firm (which may also take care of all shipping arrangements). The cost of crating depends on the dimensions, medium, and condition of the artwork. Also, museum quality crates are more expensive, since they are expected to be used multiple times. Gallery quality crating is only expected to be used once, and so is less expensive.
- *Credit card fees.* This can be a substantial amount, since many clients prefer to pay on the spot with credit cards.
- *Depreciation.* This is the periodic charge-off of fixed assets, such as equipment, furniture and fixtures, vehicles, and leasehold improvements.
- *Framing.* As noted in the discussion of inventory, the cost of framing is usually assigned to specific paintings, which means that it is capitalized into inventory. If a gallery owner chooses not to use that more theoretically correct approach, the only alternative is to charge this cost to expense as incurred.
- *Income taxes.* Depending on the form of organization, the business may have to pay income taxes. In some cases, such as an "S" corporation, responsibility for paying these taxes passes through to the owners.
- *Insurance.* A gallery contains a number of extremely high-value works of art, so of course the inventory insurance on them is correspondingly high. Insurance coverage should span the in-transit period and while works are stored in

the gallery. This coverage should include transfers to and from art fairs, and while the works are being displayed at those locations.

- *Internet listing fees.* A gallery may have a membership with one of the major art e-commerce sites, such as artnet.com or artsy.net, allowing it to post artwork for sale. The monthly fees of these sites can be quite expensive.

- *Loss on obsolete frames.* Even when taking paintings on consignment, the gallery is still responsible for framing them. When this happens, there are two situations in which the frame may not be sold. One is when the client wants to have a different frame, and the other is when the painting has not sold and the gallery wants to shift it out of inventory and send it back to the artist. In the first case, unless the unused frame can be repurposed, it is a loss to the gallery. In the second case, the frame is also a loss for the gallery.

- *Memberships.* Many gallery employees have memberships in local museums, which is not usually very expensive – unless they have memberships in *all* of the local museums.

- *Office supplies.* This involves the usual paper stock, toner cartridges, and so forth.

- *Off-site storage.* The gallery may need to pay for off-site storage for excess inventory. This can be relatively expensive, since it needs to be climate-controlled and well protected.

- *Photography.* The gallery may use an outside photographer to photograph artwork for catalogs, the gallery website, and other advertising. Alternatively, this work may be done in-house.

- *Postage.* This is the cost to issue mailings to the gallery's customer list, which can be a significant expense if it conducts a large number of exhibitions and wants to issue invitations for them.

- *Professional services.* An art gallery needs to deal with an unusually large number of professional service providers, including the following:

  o *Accountant.* Some galleries prefer to outsource their accounting to a bookkeeping service, or at least use the services of a CPA or tax advisor for their year-end reporting needs.

  o *Architect.* An architect is needed for the initial build-out, and may be called upon occasionally to reconfigure the interior space.

  o *Art handler.* Art handlers are needed to handle the customs forms required for international shipments, as well as for crating and shipment services.

  o *Attorney.* An attorney is needed to write and review consignment agreements with artists, as well as collaboration agreements with other galleries.

  o *Conservator.* A conservator may be needed to inspect, repair, or advise on a work of art (almost always for artwork acquired in the secondary market). The cost to repair a work of art should be added to its cost in inventory, rather than being charged to expense as incurred.

- o *Curator.* An independent curator may be needed to set up an exhibit; these people may be paid a flat fee, or they may collect a percentage commission on all works sold during the exhibition.
- o *Publicist.* A publicist is especially useful when a gallery wants specific coverage for upcoming exhibitions.
- o *Scholar.* A scholar may be needed for authentication services (especially important for the acquisition of artwork in the secondary market), or to write material for an exhibition or catalog.

- *Promotions.* A gallery must put on a continuing stream of art shows to present the works of favored artists. These involve not just the cost of presenting art works appropriately, but also invitations to collectors and publicity, as well as providing food and drinks to attendees.
- *Property taxes.* The pass-through of property taxes depends on the rent agreement with the landlord; if the gallery owner is required to pay it, the annual fee can be quite large.
- *Rent.* A major expense is rent, since galleries are routinely situated in high-end retail districts or in areas with large amounts of foot traffic – and nearly always in a larger city. Galleries tend to locate in these areas in order to bolster their reputations. The rents in these areas are among the highest in the region. In addition, a gallery may have warehouse space in a less-expensive part of town.
- *Shipping.* This includes the cost to ship artwork from the studio to the gallery, and from there to collectors, as well as to and from art fairs. In cases where the client is billed for shipping, these amounts are subtracted from the shipping expense.
- *Software fees.* Many galleries subscribe to software for keeping track of owned inventory and consigned inventory, as well as tracking sales, maintaining customer lists, and conducting auctions and online marketing. There is usually a monthly fee associated with this software.
- *Travel and entertainment.* There are travel and entertainment costs associated with visits to artists, customers, or dealers in other cities, as well as travel to art fairs.
- *Utilities.* This includes the usual electricity, heating, water, phone and Internet, and very definitely an alarm system – given the value of the artworks on display.
- *Wages.* Galleries are usually open more than five days a week, and may be open outside of their normal hours for preferred collectors. Someone has to be manning the shop during these hours. Everyone other than the gallery owner must be paid, so this can result in significant compensation expenses.

Artwork Contributions

A gallery may be asked to contribute an artwork, perhaps to be sold off at a charity auction. If so, the proper accounting for the transaction is to record the contribution expense at the lower of the market value of the artwork on the date of the contribution or its carrying amount.

EXAMPLE

Cold Smoke Gallery contributes a bronze sculpture produced by artist Xavier Yuri Zipinski to a local charity auction. The gallery acquired the piece for $1,000. There are many copies of the work on the market, and one of them in similar condition sold at auction a few months ago for $850. The $850 sale price reasonably approximates the fair market value of the sculpture, so the gallery takes a loss of $150 on the contribution, which its accountant records with the following entry:

	Debit	Credit
Charitable contributions (expense)	850	
Loss on LCM adjustment (expense)	150	
Inventory - xyz2020-003 (asset)		1,000

Art Gallery Fixed Assets

A *fixed asset* is property with a useful life greater than one reporting period, and which exceeds an organization's minimum capitalization limit. The *capitalization limit* is the amount paid for an asset, above which the business records it as a fixed asset. If the gallery pays less than the capitalization limit for an asset, it charges the amount to expense in the period incurred.

Art galleries invest in a relatively small amount of fixed assets. They usually lease space rather than owning it, so there is no need to account for a building. However, they will likely invest in leasehold improvements for such items as walls, lighting, a fire suppression system, and a reception area. A *leasehold improvement* is the customization of rental property. A gallery owner may also invest in a kitchen area, which could be extensive if the intent is to periodically rent out the gallery space for functions. If an architect was paid to design the gallery space, then the architect's fees are also considered to be part of the leasehold improvements. When investments have been made in leasehold improvements, the accounting for them is to amortize the expense over the lesser of the useful life of the assets or the term of the lease. In most cases, this means that the cost of the improvements should be amortized over the life of the lease. *Amortization* is the process of incrementally charging the cost of an asset to expense over its expected period of use.

EXAMPLE

Cold Smoke Gallery enters into a property lease that has a five-year term. It invests $15,000 in architectural designs, $35,000 in walls, $10,000 in lighting, and $20,000 in kitchen facilities, totaling $80,000. The related entry is:

	Debit	Credit
Fixed assets – leasehold improvements (asset)	80,000	
Cash (asset)		80,000

The useful life of these leasehold improvements is considered to be the term of the lease, which is 60 months. Accordingly, the gallery's accountant uses the following entry to charge $1,333 to expense in each of the 60 months:

	Debit	Credit
Amortization expense (expense)	1,333	
Accumulated amortization (contra asset)		1,333

In addition, a gallery will probably invest in furniture and business equipment, such as a reception desk, staff workstations, chairs, computers, printers, and copiers. As long as these expenditures exceed the capitalization limit, they are capitalized in the Furniture and Fixtures asset account. A gallery may also own a boom lift, which is used to change lights and assist with artwork installations. The cost of the lift is stated in the Equipment asset account. And finally, the firm might own a small moving van, which is used to pick up and deliver artwork. The cost of the van is stated in the Vehicles asset account.

The capitalized costs of these purchases are charged to expense over an extended period of time through ongoing depreciation. *Depreciation* is the planned, gradual reduction in the recorded value of an asset over its useful life by charging it to expense[2]. There are three factors to consider in the calculation of depreciation, which are:

- *Useful life*. This is the time period over which it is expected that an asset will be productive. Depreciation is recognized over the useful life of an asset. Rather than recording a different useful life for every individual asset, it is easier to assign each asset to an asset class, such as furniture and fixtures, where every asset in that asset class has the same useful life. Useful lives can vary significantly by asset class. For example, the useful life of all assets stored in the furniture and fixtures account may be set at seven years, while the lives for everything in the equipment account is 10 years, and all vehicles are set at five years.

---

[2] The depreciation term is used for tangible assets, while amortization is used for intangible assets and leasehold improvements.

- *Salvage value.* When a gallery eventually disposes of an asset, it may be able to sell the asset for some reduced amount, which is its salvage value. Depreciation is calculated based on the asset cost, less any estimated salvage value. If salvage value is expected to be quite small, it is generally ignored for the purpose of calculating depreciation.
- *Depreciation method.* Depreciation expense can be calculated using the straight-line method or an accelerated method that results in more depreciation expense early in the life of an asset. Galleries generally use the straight-line method when calculating depreciation for their financial statements. An accelerated method may be used for tax reporting purposes.

Under the straight-line method of depreciation, recognize depreciation expense evenly over the estimated useful life of an asset. The straight-line calculation steps are:

1. Subtract the estimated salvage value of the asset from the amount at which it is recorded on the books.
2. Determine the estimated useful life of the asset.
3. Divide the estimated useful life (in years) into 1 to arrive at the straight-line depreciation rate.
4. Multiply the depreciation rate by the asset cost (less salvage value).

EXAMPLE

Optimistic Gallery purchases a $40,000 light truck and estimates that its salvage value will be $10,000 in five years, when the owner plans to dispose of the asset. This means that Optimistic will depreciate $30,000 of the asset cost over five years, leaving $10,000 of the cost remaining at the end of that time. Its calculation of straight-line depreciation for the light truck is as follows:

1. Purchase cost of $40,000 – Estimated salvage value of $10,000 = Depreciable asset cost of $30,000

2. $1 \div 5$-Year useful life = 20% Depreciation rate per year

3. 20% Depreciation rate × $30,000 Depreciable asset cost = $6,000 Annual depreciation

---

EXAMPLE

Cold Smoke Gallery has purchased a moving van for $45,000, a boom lift for $15,000, and a reception desk for $2,000. The related entry is:

	Debit	Credit
Fixed assets – equipment (asset)	15,000	
Fixed assets – furniture and fixtures (asset)	2,000	
Fixed assets – vehicles (asset)	45,000	
Cash (asset)		62,000

The accountant assigns a useful life of five years to the van, 10 years to the lift, and seven years to the desk, which results in monthly depreciation charges on these items of $750, $125, and $24, respectively. This results in the following journal entry:

	Debit	Credit
Depreciation expense (expense)	899	
Accumulated depreciation (contra asset)		899

Art Gallery Payables

Accounts payable refers to the collective obligation to pay suppliers for goods and services that were acquired on credit. The day-to-day accounting for accounts payable is relatively simple. Whenever the gallery receives an invoice from a supplier, the accountant enters the vendor number of the supplier into the accounting software, which automatically assigns a default general ledger account number from the vendor master file to the invoice. The vendor master file contains essential information about each supplier, including a default account number to which it is assumed that most invoices from that supplier will be charged.

EXAMPLE

Blue Sky Gallery receives an invoice from Mary Aleppo, which provides the gallery with photography services. In the vendor master file, the accountant has already assigned general ledger account number 6150, Photography Fees, to Ms. Aleppo. Thus, when the accountant enters the invoice into the accounts payable module of the accounting software, the system automatically assigns the invoice to account 6150.

If the invoice is for goods or services other than the predetermined general ledger account number, the accountant can manually enter a different account number, which is only good for that specific invoice – it does not become the new default account for the supplier. In short, the pre-assignment of account numbers to suppliers greatly simplifies the accounting for payables.

The accounting software should automatically create a credit to the accounts payable account whenever the accountant records a supplier invoice. Thus, a typical entry might be:

	Debit	Credit
Rent expense (expense account)	xxx	
Accounts payable (liability account)		xxx

Later, when the gallery pays suppliers (typically during a weekly check run), the accounting system eliminates the accounts payable balance with the following entry:

	Debit	Credit
Accounts payable (liability account)	xxx	
Cash (asset account)		xxx

It is possible that small debit or credit residual balances may appear in the accounts payable account. These balances may be caused by any number of issues, such as credit memos[3] issued by suppliers which the gallery accountant does not plan to use, or amounts that the gallery had valid cause not to pay. Occasionally run the aged accounts payable report to spot these items; it looks very much like the accounts receivable aging report, except that it contains unpaid payables. Do not use journal entries to clear them out, since this will not be recognized by the report writing software that generates the aged accounts payable report. Instead, always create debit or credit memo transactions that are recognized by the report writer; this will flush the residual balances from the aged accounts payable report.

There is usually an option in the accounting software that automatically generates the necessary credit memo. As an example, a gallery may have been granted a credit memo by a supplier for $100, to be used to reduce the amount of an outstanding account payable. The accountant enters the credit memo screen in the accounting software, enters the name of the supplier and the credit memo amount, and selects the expense account that will be offset. The journal entry that the software automatically generates could be as follows:

	Debit	Credit
Accounts payable (liability account)	100	
Promotions expense (expense account)		100

---

[3] A credit memo is a contraction of the term "credit memorandum," which is a document issued by the seller of goods or services to the buyer, reducing the amount that the buyer owes to the seller under the terms of an earlier invoice.

If a supplier offers a discount in exchange for the early payment of an invoice, the gallery is not paying the full amount of the invoice. Instead, that portion of the invoice related to the discount is charged to a separate account. If an accounting software package is used, the system automatically allocates the appropriate amount to this separate account. For example, an entry to take a 2% early payment discount on a supplier invoice might be:

	Debit	Credit
Accounts payable (liability account)	100	
Cash (asset account)		98
Discounts taken (contra expense account)		2

This entry flushes out the full amount of the original account payable, so that no residual balance remains in the accounting records to be paid.

The Chart of Accounts

The chart of accounts is a list that states every account in the general ledger[4]. The chart usually begins with all asset accounts, followed by liability accounts, equity accounts, revenue accounts, and finally expense accounts. The following table contains a sample chart of accounts for an art gallery, and includes an account number, account name, and account type. The accounts used in the table will not exactly match the needs of every gallery, but indicate the types of accounts that should be employed.

Sample Chart of Accounts

Account Number	Account Name	Account Type
1000	Cash – checking account	Asset
1010	Cash – savings account	Asset
1020	Investments	Asset
1200	Accounts receivable	Asset
1210	Allowance for doubtful accounts	Asset
1300	Prepaid expenses	Asset
1410	Inventory – paintings	Asset
1420	Inventory – sculptures	Asset
1430	Inventory – pottery	Asset
1505	Fixed assets – equipment	Asset
1510	Fixed assets – furniture and fixtures	Asset
1515	Fixed assets – leasehold improvements	Asset

---

[4] For a discussion of how the general ledger is used, see the author's *Bookkeeping Guidebook* course.

Account Number	Account Name	Account Type
1520	Fixed assets – vehicles	Asset
1530	Accumulated amortization	Asset
1540	Accumulated depreciation	Asset
1600	Other assets	Asset
2000	Accounts payable	Liability
2100	Accrued expenses	Liability
2200	Taxes payable	Liability
2300	Wages payable	Liability
2400	Other liabilities	Liability
2500	Notes payable	Liability
3000	Common stock	Equity
3100	Additional paid-in capital	Equity
3200	Retained earnings	Equity
4100	Revenue – paintings	Revenue
4200	Revenue – sculptures	Revenue
4300	Revenue – pottery	Revenue
4400	Revenue – catalogs	Revenue
4500	Revenue – repair brokering	Revenue
4600	Revenue – commissions	Revenue
4700	Revenue – framing	Revenue
4800	Revenue – home delivery and hanging	Revenue
4900	Revenue – space rental	Revenue
5000	Cost of goods – owned artwork	Expense
5100	Cost of goods – catalogs	Expense
5200	Cost of goods – crating	Expense
5300	Cost of goods – repair fees	Expense
5400	Cost of goods – consignment commissions	Expense
5500	Cost of goods – framing	Expense
6000	Advertising expense	Expense
6010	Art advisor fees	Expense
6020	Art fairs expense	Expense
6030	Artist per diems	Expense
6040	Artist stipends	Expense
6050	Banking fees	Expense
6060	Benefits	Expense
6070	Charitable contributions	Expense

Account Number	Account Name	Account Type
6080	Credit card fees	Expense
6090	Depreciation expense	Expense
6100	Insurance expense	Expense
6110	Internet listing fees	Expense
6120	Memberships expense	Expense
6130	Office supplies expense	Expense
6140	Off-site storage fees	Expense
6150	Photography fees	Expense
6160	Postage expense	Expense
6170	Professional services expense	Expense
6180	Promotions expense	Expense
6190	Property taxes	Expense
6200	Rent expense	Expense
6210	Shipping expense	Expense
6220	Software fees	Expense
6230	Travel and entertainment	Expense
6240	Utilities expense	Expense
6250	Wages expense	Expense
7000	Interest expense	Expense
7100	Income taxes expense	Expense

In those rare cases in which a gallery has a relatively large number of staff, it may be useful to develop a more refined chart of accounts, so that expenses can be aggregated by department. These departments are likely to be artist relations, operations, press, sales, and finance and administration. When these departments are added, the key difference in the chart of accounts is to the expense line items, where some line items may be duplicated for several departments. This information can then be used to aggregate information into departmental financial statements. A sample chart of accounts (just for expenses) that incorporates departments appears in the following exhibit.

Sample Chart of Accounts

Account Number	Account Name	Account Type
6000	Advertising expense – press	Expense
6010	Art advisor fees – sales	Expense
6020	Art fairs expense – sales	Expense
6030	Artist per diems – artist relations	Expense
6040	Artist stipends – artist relations	Expense
6050	Banking fees – finance	Expense
6060	Benefits – artist relations	Expense
6061	Benefits – operations	Expense
6062	Benefits – press	Expense
6063	Benefits – sales	Expense
6064	Benefits – finance	Expense
6070	Charitable contributions – finance	Expense
6080	Credit card fees – finance	Expense
6090	Depreciation expense – finance	Expense
6100	Insurance expense – finance	Expense
6110	Internet listing fees – sales	Expense
6120	Memberships expense – press	Expense
6121	Membership expense – sales	Expense
6130	Office supplies expense – finance	Expense
6131	Office supplies expense – operations	Expense
6140	Off-site storage fees – operations	Expense
6150	Photography fees – press	Expense
6151	Photography fees – sales	Expense
6160	Postage expense – sales	Expense
6170	Professional services expense – operations	Expense
6171	Professional services expense – press	Expense
6172	Professional services expense – sales	Expense
6173	Professional services expense – finance	Expense
6180	Promotions expense – press	Expense
6181	Promotions expense – sales	Expense
6190	Property taxes – finance	Expense
6200	Rent expense – finance	Expense
6210	Shipping expense – operations	Expense
6220	Software fees – finance	Expense

Account Number	Account Name	Account Type
6230	Travel and entertainment – artist relations	Expense
6231	Travel and entertainment – press	Expense
6232	Travel and entertainment – sales	Expense
6240	Utilities expense – finance	Expense
6250	Wages expense – artist relations	Expense
6251	Wages expense – operations	Expense
6252	Wages expense – press	Expense
6253	Wages expense – sales	Expense
6254	Wages expense – finance	Expense
7000	Interest expense – finance	Expense
7100	Income taxes expense	Expense

Financial Statements

An art gallery will be called upon to periodically issue financial statements, either to its owner or to outside parties, such as lenders and creditors. The financial statements include the income statement, balance sheet, and statement of cash flows. In the following subsections, we present sample formats for each of these financial statements, presented from the perspective of an art gallery.

Income Statement

The income statement presents the results of operations for a period of time. The statement begins with revenues, from which expenses are subtracted, leaving a profit or loss at the bottom of the report. It is derived entirely from the revenue and expense accounts listed in the chart of accounts. A sample income statement follows.

Cold Smoke Gallery
Income Statement
For the Year Ended December 31, 20X1
(in thousands)

Sales	$100,000
Less: Discounts	8,000
Net sales	92,000
Cost of sales	52,000
Gross profit	40,000
Operating expenses:	
Compensation and benefits	16,000
Rent and property taxes	8,000
Promotions and fairs	5,000
Travel and entertainment	3,000
Utilities expense	1,000
Other expenses	3,000
Total operating expenses	36,000
Net profit from operations	4,000
Other income (expense):	
Interest expense, net	-1,000
Net profit before income taxes	3,000
Income tax expense	1,000
Net after-tax profit	$2,000

There is no mandated presentation for the income statement. For example, a gallery owner may choose to break down sales into more line items, as may also be the case with the expense aggregations we have chosen for this presentation. The main point is to design a layout that imparts the most information, given the financial requirements of a gallery.

Balance Sheet

The balance sheet presents the financial position of a business as of a point in time, usually the end of a month. Assets are presented first, followed by liabilities and equity. This report is useful for evaluating the liquidity of a business by comparing the size and types of its assets and liabilities. It is derived entirely from the asset, liability, and equity accounts listed in the chart of accounts. A sample balance sheet follows.

Cold Smoke Gallery
Balance Sheet
As of December 31, 20X1
(in thousands)

ASSETS	
Current assets:	
Cash and cash equivalents	$18,000
Investments	50,000
Accounts receivable	85,000
Inventories	270,000
Other current assets	4,000
Total current assets	427,000
Fixed assets	110,000
Other current assets	5,000
Total assets	$542,000
LIABILITIES AND EQUITY	
Current liabilities:	
Accounts payable	59,000
Accrued expenses	9,000
Total current liabilities	68,000
Long-term debt	60,000
Total liabilities	128,000
Stockholders' equity:	
Common stock	2,000
Additional paid-in capital	40,000
Retained earnings	372,000
Total shareholders' equity	414,000
Total liabilities and equity	$542,000

As was the case with the income statement, the balance sheet can be adjusted to present the most critical accounts. For example, the commissions payable liability account could be presented in its own line, rather than being aggregated into the accounts payable line item.

Statement of Cash Flows

The statement of cash flows presents the cash inflows and outflows associated with a business for a reporting period. These cash flows are divided into operating, investing, and financing activities. When combined with the income statement, one can discern a great deal about the financial viability of an art gallery.

Cold Smoke Gallery
Statement of Cash Flows
For the Year Ended December 31, 20X1
(in thousands)

Cash flows from operating activities:	
Net profit	$2,000
Adjustments to reconcile net profit to net cash provided by operating activities:	
Depreciation and amortization	1,000
Changes in operating assets and liabilities, net:	
Accounts receivable	32,000
Inventories	-17,000
Other current assets	-3,000
Accounts payable	14,000
Accrued expenses	-1,000
Net cash provided by operating activities	28,000
Cash flows from investing activities:	
Acquisition of property and equipment	-11,000
Proceeds from sale of assets	0
Net cash used in investing activities	-11,000
Cash flows from financing activities:	
Proceeds from long-term debt	0
Payments on long-term debt	-3,000
Net cash used in financing activities	-3,000
Net change in cash and cash equivalents	14,000
Cash and cash equivalents at beginning of year	4,000
Cash and cash equivalents at end of year	$18,000

To learn more about the evaluation of financial statements, see the author's *Interpretation of Financial Statements* book.

Form 8300 Filings

The United States government wants to be notified when large amounts of cash are used to pay for works of art. Accordingly, a gallery is required to submit a Form 8300, *Report of Cash Payments over $10,000 Received in a Trade or Business*, to the Internal Revenue Service when this happens. The specific IRS requirements relating to this form are:

> Each person engaged in a trade or business who, in the course of that trade or business, receives more than $10,000 in cash in one transaction or in two or more related transactions, must file Form 8300. Any transactions conducted between a payer (or its agent) and the recipient in a 24-hour period are related transactions. Transactions are considered related even if they occur over a period of more than 24 hours if the recipient knows, or has reason to know, that each transaction is one of a series of connected transactions.

One should file a Form 8300 by the 15th day after the date when the cash was received. It should then be filed with the IRS at the following address:

Detroit Computing Center

P.O. Box 32621

Detroit, MI 48232

A sample of the first page of the Form 8300 appears on the following page.

Sample Form 8300

IRS Form **8300** (Rev. August 2014) Department of the Treasury Internal Revenue Service	**Report of Cash Payments Over $10,000 Received in a Trade or Business** ▶ See instructions for definition of cash. ▶ Use this form for transactions occurring after August 29, 2014. Do not use prior versions after this date. For Privacy Act and Paperwork Reduction Act Notice, see the last page.	FinCEN Form **8300** (Rev. August 2014) OMB No. 1506-0018 Department of the Treasury Financial Crimes Enforcement Network

1 Check appropriate box(es) if: **a** ☐ Amends prior report;   **b** ☐ Suspicious transaction.

Part I   **Identity of Individual From Whom the Cash Was Received**

2 If more than one individual is involved, check here and see instructions . . . . ▶ ☐

3 Last name	**4** First name	**5** M.I.	**6** Taxpayer identification number

7 Address (number, street, and apt. or suite no.)	**8** Date of birth . . . ▶ M M D D Y Y Y Y (see instructions)

9 City	**10** State	**11** ZIP code	**12** Country (if not U.S.)	**13** Occupation, profession, or business

14 Identifying document (ID)   **a** Describe ID ▶   **c** Number ▶   **b** Issued by ▶

Part II   **Person on Whose Behalf This Transaction Was Conducted**

15 If this transaction was conducted on behalf of more than one person, check here and see instructions . . . . ▶ ☐

16 Individual's last name or organization's name	**17** First name	**18** M.I.	**19** Taxpayer identification number

20 Doing business as (DBA) name (see instructions)	Employer identification number

21 Address (number, street, and apt. or suite no.)	**22** Occupation, profession, or business

23 City	**24** State	**25** ZIP code	**26** Country (if not U.S.)

27 Alien identification (ID)   **a** Describe ID ▶   **c** Number ▶   **b** Issued by ▶

Part III   **Description of Transaction and Method of Payment**

28 Date cash received M M D D Y Y Y Y	**29** Total cash received $ .00	**30** If cash was received in more than one payment, check here . . ▶ ☐	**31** Total price if different from item 29 $ .00

32 Amount of cash received (in U.S. dollar equivalent) (must equal item 29) (see instructions):

a U.S. currency	$ .00	(Amount in $100 bills or higher $ .00)
b Foreign currency	$ .00	(Country ▶)
c Cashier's check(s)	$ .00	Issuer's name(s) and serial number(s) of the monetary instrument(s) ▶
d Money order(s)	$ .00	
e Bank draft(s)	$ .00	
f Traveler's check(s)	$ .00	

33 Type of transaction

a ☐ Personal property purchased	**f** ☐ Debt obligations paid	**34** Specific description of property or service shown in 33. Give serial or registration number, address, docket number, etc. ▶
b ☐ Real property purchased	**g** ☐ Exchange of cash	
c ☐ Personal services provided	**h** ☐ Escrow or trust funds	
d ☐ Business services provided	**i** ☐ Bail received by court clerks	
e ☐ Intangible property purchased	**j** ☐ Other (specify in item 34) ▶	

Part IV   **Business That Received Cash**

35 Name of business that received cash	**36** Employer identification number

37 Address (number, street, and apt. or suite no.)	Social security number

38 City	**39** State	**40** ZIP code	**41** Nature of your business

42 Under penalties of perjury, I declare that to the best of my knowledge the information I have furnished above is true, correct, and complete.

Signature ▶ _____ Authorized official   Title ▶ _____

43 Date of signature M M D D Y Y Y Y	**44** Type or print name of contact person	**45** Contact telephone number

IRS Form **8300** (Rev. 8-2014)   Cat. No. 62133S   FinCEN Form **8300** (Rev. 8-2014)

Art Gallery Metrics

A massive cause of the success of art galleries is the networking ability of their employees, and especially of their owner(s). These individuals are constantly searching for new artists to present to their clients, attending art fairs to meet new clients, and engaging in ongoing communications with existing clients, as well as other dealers. These activities are extremely difficult to translate into performance metrics. Nonetheless, we have come up with a few measures that may be of use, which are:

- *Conversion rate.* Many people may walk in the door, but few are willing to purchase. Of those who enter the premises, some are casually passing by, others are art enthusiasts but have little interest in buying, and others are interested in viewing shows – but are there mostly for the socializing and less to buy anything. Only collectors are really interested in buying, and they comprise a small fraction of the total number entering the gallery. Consequently, it can be useful to compare the number of buyers to the number of gallery visitors. Galleries rarely count their foot traffic, so a reasonable substitute is to count them just for a few time blocks during the month, to gain an approximation of total foot traffic.
- *Sales per square foot.* In some locations, rent is *extremely* expensive. When this is the case, consider comparing the net sales each month to the square footage of the gallery, and track the result on a trend line. If the trend is downward, it might make sense to look for additional revenue sources or shift to a less-expensive location.
- *Profitability of art fairs.* The total cost of the typical art fair is very high, given the cost of booth rental, travel and entertainment, freight costs, and so forth. That being the case, it makes sense to subtract all art fair costs from the resulting sales (net of commissions), to see if the gallery is really making any money on these activities.

Art Gallery Best Practices

The most profitable art galleries consistently exhibit the same practices, which leads us to recommend the following best practices for those desiring to obtain exceptional profitability:

- *Develop a brand.* Collectors need to be put in a position where they trust the judgment of a favored gallery, thereby linking them tightly to the gallery and its artworks. Branding involves having high-quality exhibitions, strong curation, and customer service. Another area of focus is communications, where collectors are targeted with only the artists and types of art for which they have expressed an interest.
- *Employ full-timers.* Having a reasonably well-paid and well-educated staff strongly correlates with more sales. The reason is that attentive employees generate more sales, whereas an indifferent part-timer generates minimal sales. This also means that the pay structure should involve a relatively low base pay, combined with a robust commission incentive that encourages the staff to sell.
- *Move away from the high rent district.* The principal buyers of art are art collectors, who have no particular interest in where a gallery is located. A

location in a high-rent district tends to attract much more foot traffic, but this traffic does not include many art collectors, who are more interested in easy access to parking within walking distance of the gallery.

- *Focus tightly on collectors.* The gallery should focus nearly all of its efforts on identified collectors. Everyone else who enters the gallery can be ignored, since their purchases comprise only a small part of the total. It can make sense to open new locations near clusters of collectors.
- *Develop multi-channel sales.* A gallery owner must be willing to sell through partners, art fairs, and on-line – essentially using any practical distribution channel – rather than relying on one or two fixed retail locations. These other approaches are more likely to bring in entirely new collectors.
- *Deal in the secondary market.* There is a strong market for the resale of works by established artists, so a gallery should work to gain access to this market, selling these works to its stable of collectors. A particular benefit is that the works are already well-known, so they command high prices and are readily sold off. In addition, investors are most interested in these works, which expands the group of collectors.

Summary

The operating characteristics of an art gallery present special challenges for the accountant. The most obvious item is the revenue split between the gallery and the artist, resulting in a massive amount of gallery sales immediately being lost to the artist commission. Another concern is tracking costs that have been capitalized into inventory (especially when investing in secondary market purchases), since this represents a massive chunk of a gallery's working capital investment. And finally, the increasing proportion of expenditures for art fairs would lead the accountant to structure the reporting system to track revenues and expenses by art fair, in order to determine which ones are profitable – or not.

Glossary

A

Accounts payable. The collective obligation to pay suppliers for goods and services that were acquired on credit.

Amortization. The process of incrementally charging the cost of an asset to expense over its expected period of use.

Art gallery. An outlet through which works of art are marketed.

B

Balance sheet. A report that presents the financial position of a business as of a point in time.

C

Capitalization limit. The amount paid for an asset, above which the business records it as a fixed asset.

Chart of accounts. A list that states every account in the general ledger.

D

Depreciation. The planned, gradual reduction in the recorded value of an asset over its useful life by charging it to expense.

E

Economic nexus. When a business generates a certain amount of sales in a particular state.

F

Fixed asset. Property with a useful life greater than one reporting period, and which exceeds an organization's minimum capitalization limit.

G

General ledger. The master set of accounts that summarize all transactions occurring within a business.

I

Income statement. A report that presents the financial results of a business for a stated period of time.

Invoice. A document submitted to a client, identifying a sale transaction for which the client owes payment to the gallery.

J

Journal entry. A formalized method for recording a business transaction.

L

Leasehold improvement. The customization of rental property.

N

Nexus. The physical presence of a business in a state.

S

Sales tax. A tax imposed on the sale of tangible personal property and certain services.

Salvage value. The expected price at which an asset can be sold at the end of its useful life.

Secondary market. The sale of artwork between collectors, rather than from the originating artist.

Specific identification method. An inventory tracking system that uniquely identifies and tracks each item in stock.

Statement of cash flows. A report that presents the cash inflows and outflows associated with a business for a stated period of time.

U

Useful life. The time period over which a fixed asset is expected to be productive.

Index